This book was presented to

Donna Frroku

of

RSPCA Blackberry Farm Animal Centre

in

2007

To mark an outstanding effort and personal achievement whilst under training

This award was made possible by the generosity of Mrs Jeanne McBride; long time Auxiliary for Beverley and Hon. Secretary of the Hull and East Riding Branch, as her way of recognising the otherwise largely unrewarded efforts of staff At the RSPCA's Animal Centres

TEACHING A PARROT TO TALK

Elaine Radford

Distributed in the UNITED STATES to the Pet Trade by T.F.H. Publications, Inc., 1 TFH Plaza, Neptune City, NJ 07753; on the Internet at www.tfh.com; in CANADA by Rolf C. Hagen Inc., 3225 Sartelon St., Montreal, Quebec H4R 1E8; Pet Trade by H & L Pet Supplies Inc., 27 Kingston Crescent, Kitchener, Ontario N2B 2T6; in ENGLAND by T.F.H. Publications, PO Box 74, Havant PO9 5TT; in AUSTRALIA AND THE SOUTH PACIFIC by T.F.H. (Australia), Pty. Ltd., Box 149, Brookvale 2100 N.S.W., Australia; in NEW ZEALAND by Brooklands Aquarium Ltd., 5 McGiven Drive, New Plymouth, RD1 New Zealand; in SOUTH AFRICA by Rolf C. Hagen S.A. (PTY.) LTD., P.O. Box 201199, Durban North 4016, South Africa; in JAPAN by T.F.H. Publications. Published by T.F.H. Publications, Inc.

MANUFACTURED IN THE
UNITED STATES OF AMERICA
BY T.F.H. PUBLICATIONS, INC.

Contents

Photography by:
Herbert R. Axelrod, Joan Balzarini, Isabelle Francais, Michael Gilroy, Robert Pearcy, John Tyson, Louise B. Van der Meid. Special thanks to Nancy's Parrot Sanctuary and Lena Dodson

Teaching your parrot to talk is an ideal way to build a trusting and enjoyable relationship between you and your pet.

THE MYSTIQUE OF THE TALKING PARROT

The Yellow-Crowned Amazon considered the crowd of neighbors that had gathered at the garage sale. As my partner and I discussed the feasibility of purchasing the talented bird, I pointed out that we didn't have any cash on hand at the moment. The Amazon was quick to speak up. "Gotta credit card?" he asked in a sweet, insinuating voice.

Moments later, the owner returned from ringing up another sale. We told him what the parrot had said. The owner was skeptical, since he'd had the bird for several years and had never heard him use that phrase. Everyone else agreed that the bird had made the statement, in as clear a human voice as anyone might wish. Before the owner could comment further, the Amazon himself chimed in, repeating in a more insistent tone, "Gotta credit card?"

Stunned, the owner could only stammer that he didn't accept credit cards.

To this day (we later returned and bought him with cash), the gifted Yellow-Crown can come up with an appropriate comment for certain situations—but only if he wants to. Most of the time he chatters away out of sheer high spirits, wishing himself "Happy Birthday!" at random and greeting himself with his favorite phrase in the world, "Hello, Cookie!" Yet, ever so often, he'll drop in a remark that's so apropos that you can't help but wonder about the hidden wheels turning within his avian brain. For example, when we traveled to the beach, after observing the sand and several brown pelicans, he proudly told a passerby that "I gotta go." When they asked where he was going, he announced, "Gotta go to Florida." In fact, we were not in Florida, but it seemed like a pretty good guess for a parrot.

Yellow-Crowned Amazons are among the many different parrots that exhibit talking abilities.

What is it about a talking bird that seems to bring some of the ancient fairy tale magic back into the world? I've seen people stop dead in their tracks to ask if a chattering parrot was really doing the talking or if there was some kind of electronic device involved. Listening to a small, feathered creature speak, even if the words are mostly nonsense, awakens a childlike sense of wonder that makes us believe, if only for a moment, in a world of marvels and mystery. On those special occasions when the words do make sense, the magic is intensified.

Because of their near-mystical gift for human speech and their sometimes uncanny ability to say the right thing at the right time, parrots have been cherished by kings and queens for thousands of years. In the last few centuries, and especially the last decade, there has been an explosion of knowledge about how to breed, care for, and train the various talented members of the parrot family. You no longer have to conquer an empire like Alexander the Great did to be presented with a rare talking bird. Instead, if you take the time to educate yourself about your pet, you too can possess one of these talented treasures.

There has also been a revolutionary change in our understanding of the parrot brain. In the past, experts insisted that no talking bird could understand what it was

Some species, though not noted for their speech skills, hold surprises; young birds, especially, can be trained to talk from an early age.

Considered by many to be the most talented of talkers, the African Grey (Congo African shown) is often chosen as a pet for this reason.

saying and that it was simply a coincidence if the animal happened to come out with the occasional intelligent remark. Those who observed that the "coincidences" happened quite often were simply dismissed as sentimental or even weak-minded. Over the past two decades, however, Dr. Irene Pepperberg and her associates have dedicated themselves to the task of demonstrating that a properly trained parrot can comprehend what it's saying and actively utilize the English language to communicate with humans.

The star of Pepperberg's training program is an ordinary African Grey named Alex, who was purchased in a Chicago pet store in 1977. Anyone who has seen Alex on television or read transcripts of his interviews with various reporters can only be impressed with how far a bird brain can go. Granted, he isn't ready to give advice on world events, but he can count, name colors, answer questions, ask for what he wants, and even tell interviewers to "go away" when he's had enough. To be perfectly honest, his conversations may often be more intelligent than what a lot of us have to listen to at an average business lunch.

Although I can't promise that your talking bird will be giving interviews on television, I hope to provide some clues

Researchers have demonstrated that properly trained parrots, African Greys in particular, can comprehend language and communicate with humans.

Not all African Greys become exceptionally talkative; the only real guarantee is to find one that already speaks.

Whereas humans generate sound with larynx, tongue, and lips, birds use syrinx muscles to control the sounds they make.

that will help you develop your parrot's talents to the best of your ability. I say *your* ability, rather than your *parrot's* ability, because it is up to you to put in the time and effort required to choose the right bird and then to educate him properly. Few of us are in a position to make training a bird to talk a full-time career, so we must be realistic about the time and energy that we can devote to the project. I will tell you upfront that some birds will never talk, for a variety of reasons that we'll explore later. You must be emotionally prepared to accept your parrot for what he is, even if he's the strong silent type, and also to accept yourself for what you are, if you decide that quiet companionship is more to your liking than another talking lesson at the end of the day. A talking parrot is meant to be a pleasure, not a second job. If you and your bird aren't having fun along the way, there's something wrong.

WHY DO PARROTS TALK?

Before we start training our parrots, we need to have a good idea of what motivates them to speak up. The avian voicebox is quite different from the human voicebox, which is a condition that doesn't make forming human words any easier. As you may know, human voice originates in the larynx, where the throat meets the windpipe. If you place your hand on your throat, you can feel a buzz in your larynx whenever you talk. We also use our tongue and lips to modify sounds that come from our larynx, allowing us greater control over our pronunciation and permitting us to employ a larger number of words.

By contrast, a bird's voice originates from the syrinx, located between the bottom end of the windpipe and the two bronchial tubes leading to the lungs. Instead of using

Although your pet may speak in order to greet you, parrots in the wild use their natural cries to warn of danger or call to mates.

Parrots use their own "language" of vocalizations to bond with members of their flock.

their tongues to modify sounds, birds must develop exquisite control of their syrinx muscles to create the sounds they want. The syrinx muscles may be more developed in some species of birds than others, granting different species differing abilities to vocalize.

Given their proven performance, it would be perfectly natural to assume that parrots have the most well-developed syrinxes of any birds. Surprisingly enough, this assumption is quite wrong. The most complex and advanced voiceboxes are found in the large group of birds known as the songbirds, which includes birds such as the brown thrasher, a bird that can actually sing two notes at once. Some birds, such as crows and starlings, have displayed a talent for talking and mimicry that rivals that of the parrots. I've even speculated that a properly trained crow or mynah might be able to hold his own with Alex.

In any case, even without the advanced songbird syrinx, parrots can and do manage to learn to talk, often quite well. I don't believe that they do it just for the sheer joy of sounding off, either, since they can get just as much pleasure from shrieking nonverbally if they so desire. There are perfectly good reasons why a parrot might wish to learn to speak, and if we understand those reasons, we'll have a better chance of encouraging a given bird to explore its talent for talk.

Birds in the wild vocalize for a variety of reasons. We are all familiar with songbirds, which sing to claim territory and to impress females. In some species, females may also sing in order to warn off their rivals. Parrots, of course, are not songbirds, and their natural cries tend to be harsh and strident rather than musical. In general, however, they are extremely social birds that call back and forth to keep in touch with the flock or with their mates. There are special cries to indicate "Danger!" or "I'm OK. Where are you?" Some vocalizations may be instinctive, but it appears that others are learned from the parents—and we, as parrot owners, can take advantage of this learning ability to teach our parrots to speak in our own tongue.

When parrots bond with their owners, they seem to experience the same affection and concern for their special human that they would for an avian parent, mate, or flock member. Just as parrots in

Have patience—a good deal of what your parrot says at first may be mindless chatter.

the wild will call back and forth to each other to make sure that all is well and no one has spotted any predators or dangers, the captive parrot will wish to call back and forth to his owner. These calls contain about as much content as the average "How ya doing?" between neighbors, in that they give everyone a chance to touch base and make sure the flock (or neighborhood) is running smoothly. A certain amount of happy, mindless chatter is reassuring to the parrot, letting the bird know that everything's on track. Breeders who talk to their babies while handfeeding them have reported that some baby parrots have actually learned to say a few words even before weaning, as a natural result of their wish to respond to their "parent's" reassurances.

Because parrots can learn, instead of just reacting according to pre-programmed instincts, they will often observe that talking is a great way to attract attention to themselves. Many times I've

Budgies, especially those that are trained young, display an astonishing ability to pick up the human language.

walked into a room occupied by a parrot, only to have the bird immediately wolf whistle or call out a loud "Hello," to make sure that he, the most important creature in the area, wasn't overlooked. If I'm talking about something else and don't say "Hello" back immediately, the bird's calls will generally get louder and more insistent. "Hello, Hello, HELLO!" Not all parrots wish to show off for strangers, but those who do fully expect your attention and admiration.

Other parrots may actually chatter to themselves for reassurance or personal entertainment. Many people have reported on the frustrating phenomenon of the secret talker, a parrot that speaks only when there's no one in the room and whose linguistic exploits have to be enjoyed with the help of a hidden tape recorder. It's rather difficult to understand why a parrot that isn't interested in attention, praise, and food gifts would be motivated to learn to talk. Perhaps there's something comforting in being able to take on the role of being the "parent" when there's no caring human actually in the room. In any case, you need to be aware of this possibility, because some of you may already own "silent" parrots that are actually chattering away behind your back. In a later chapter, we'll explore ways of encouraging such bashful babblers to speak up.

Food treats as well as praise are an important part of encouraging your pet to talk.

Birds kept in groups are less likely to use speech to communicate with humans than birds that are kept alone, without avian companionship.

Finally, wild parrots do communicate to get important information across, such as the location of a source of food or water or the status of one's social position in the flock. When they communicate naturally, they use body language as well as calls to get their point across, and some pet parrots are content to communicate with their humans the same way. (You'll be astonished at how good you get at reading avian "body talk" after a few weeks of being owned by a new parrot.) However, research like Dr. Pepperberg's and the experience of many bird owners demonstrate that you can also teach your bird to use your own language to communicate with you. With some effort on your part, your bird can learn to greet you when you come home and to let you know when he's interested in food or water or even just love and attention.

SELECTING A PARROT THAT WILL TALK

Do you want a one hundred percent proven method for getting a parrot that will talk, first time, every time? Well, you're not going to get one. I cannot guarantee that your bird will talk, even if you do everything right, and I would be surprised if anyone else could either. Parrots are individuals, with different talents and interests, and no one really knows why it is that certain birds will instantly be attracted to the notion of talking and take to it almost from the egg, while others from supposedly gifted species stubbornly refuse to utter a word. The only way to be certain that your bird will talk in advance is to purchase a parrot that somebody else has already trained to talk.

It is up to the individual to decide how important it is to possess a bird that talks. My primary motivation for becoming involved with parrots was their beauty, intelligence, and spirit. The closest relationship I have ever had with a bird was with a non-speaking parrot, and he communicated everything he had to say in a language just as clear as spoken words. As far as I'm concerned, speech is a nice bonus in a parrot, but it is not the basis of my relationship with my pets. Indeed, if you put too much pressure on the bird to talk, it may be to the detriment of a relaxed relationship with your parrot. I would tend to suggest that if you believe you will love your parrot less if he never talks, you should reconsider the idea of owning a parrot.

However, as I said before, there is certainly something magical about a talking animal. If your heart is absolutely set on a talking parrot, the least stressful option is to find a bird that already knows how to speak. In the past, this task could be rather difficult, since owners of talking birds were unlikely to let them go for a reasonable price. (I was able to obtain Cookie, the credit card wielding Yellow Crown, only because the previous owner's health problem forced the sale.) Today, luckily, there are more and more breeders who are

Beauty and talent do not necessarily go hand-in-hand. Be certain that you are happy with your choice of parrot, regardless of whether he ever speaks.

Cockatoos, though not noted for their talking abilities, are much loved for their companionship and displays of affection.

handfeeding the popular species, and you may well be fortunate enough to be offered a baby parrot that has already learned a few words. If you can obtain a domestic-bred bird that is imprinted on humans and is already attempting to mimic our speech, you have a great candidate for talk training.

When selecting a parrot, the most important criterion is good health. Sick birds don't feel up to talking or singing, because Mother Nature tells them to conserve their energies for the healing process. I would strongly advise you to get an avian veterinarian's approval before finalizing the purchase of any parrot. There have been significant advances in medical care for birds over the past few years, including the development of some very valuable vaccines. A vet check could go a long way toward getting you and your feathered friend started on the right foot.

Another important criterion is the age of the bird. In general, the younger the bird, the better. Although parrots have adaptable brains and can keep learning throughout their lives, they are much more likely to be open to language learning if they have received exposure to it from the beginning. Today's domestic-bred babies will probably end up out-talking previous generations of wild-caught birds, although no one will deny that certain individual wild-caught birds have proven to be very gifted indeed. I am firmly convinced that Budgerigars (often called "parakeets" in pet stores in the United States, although they are not

A Peach-Front Conure, if trained properly and diligently from an early age, can develop talking skills to rival some of the more noted talkers such as African Greys and Amazons.

Double Yellowhead Amazons do not develop their full coloration until maturity. As with other parrots, they are best trained young.

A bird's color and personality, such as that of this Sun Conure, may help him to overcome his lack of exceptional talking skills.

the only kind of parakeet) are best tamed and trained while they are still young enough to have black bars on their crowns. Older Budgerigars, particularly females, can be almost impossible for the amateur to tame.

I also believe that you must work with one bird at a time if you want to have the best chance of teaching your parrot to talk. There are many breeders and trainers who would disagree, because they've been able to teach multiple birds or even an entire hatch to speak at one time. However, these people are experts, with a long history of working with parrots. Most of us have other responsibilities and are going to find it enough of a challenge to tune into one parrot in order to develop a good working relationship with that bird. Two or more parrots at a time would simply be overwhelming. There is also the risk that the multiple parrots will prefer to communicate with each other, in their own language, and that therefore none of them will become interested in talking to you.

Besides, you should want more from your parrot than just an ability to talk. You should want love and affection, and the best way to develop that bond is through one-on-one contact. Your parrot might not feel the same urgency for your attention when he can flirt with the other parrot and get its attention on demand. Some people even advise against you permitting the parrot to see himself in a mirror. Some parrots, particularly Budgerigars, will actually develop a flirtatious relationship with their own reflections. Owners have observed Budgies attempting to feed their reflection, then angrily bashing the mirror when the "other" bird refuses to respond. This sort of thing tends to detract from a serious attachment between a bird and his owner.

For most color varieties of budgies, the cere changes color as a bird matures, turning blue for a male bird and brown for a female.

A sick bird is unlikely to be interested in talking. Have your avian vet examine any bird you are considering buying.

Many bird-keepers have found that birds kept in pairs may be more interested in communicating with each other than with humans.

Although this issue often incites controversy, I believe that there are certain species that are better candidates for voice lessons than others. The staff of *Bird Talk* magazine has collected several informal reader surveys over the years and, although the results do not claim to be scientific, they suggest that certain types of parrots are better talkers than others. Since their readers picked the same species that generations of bird trainers have acclaimed as the most talented, I tend to think there's some validity to it. But let me emphasize that there is no guarantee that any individual of these species will necessarily be an avian genius. Many African Greys do not speak words at all, other than a low threatening growl, and there is even a rumor that there is a quiet Yellow-Crowned Amazon out there somewhere.

However, just because you have a certain species that is not listed, don't assume that your parrot is incapable of talking. For example, based on my experience alone, I would tend to assume that Peach-Front Conures are poor talkers, because none of my mine have ever exhibited the faintest interest in speech. However, I allow my Conures to raise their own young, rather than handfeeding them, because I'm more interested in rearing them as future breeders. Other breeders, who hand-feed their Conures to make better pets,

Though not noted to be chatterboxes, cockatiels still prove to be popular and long-lasting companion pets.

Singing, talking, and mimicry are among the many talents of African Greys, both the Congo and the Timneh subspecies.

Scientifically formulated and balanced avian diets that are made with only the finest and freshest ingredients are designed for your parrot and are available in many bird shops and pet stores. Photo courtesy of Sunshine Bird Supplies.

report that their babies can and do learn to talk. It's all a matter of training and focus.

With the understanding that this list is an admitted generalization, let's look at the parrot species that are usually considered to be the very best talkers. If you have the choice and you are serious about teaching a bird to talk, you may want to consider one of these options.

AFRICAN GREYS—AVIAN EINSTEINS?

Many people believe that African Greys (*Psittacus erithacus*) are the most intelligent birds. My personal belief is that, with more research, we will discover that we share this planet with several species of intelligent birds. However, there is little funding available for such specialized research. In any case, Dr. Pepperberg's work suggests that Greys are as intelligent or perhaps more intelligent than many of our primate relatives. To many, Alex's grasp of grammar appears superior to the sign language usage attributed to gorillas and chimpanzees, which often seem to use words in any order. Granted, Alex says, "Gotta," but so do plenty of humans.

In any case, ordinary people, not just university professors, have trained Greys to speak dozens and sometimes hundreds of words and phrases, and many proud owners report that their pets have some understanding of what they are saying. In addition to a fantastic learning capacity, most Greys have wonderfully flexible voices, and they can learn to talk like their owner, cry like the baby, meow like the cat, and beep like the microwave. Many Greys also enjoy learning to sing. Their gift for mimicry can be uncanny, to the point where you can find it difficult to tell if it was really the bird or another person in the home who called to you.

There are two subspecies of African Greys, the Congo

Be patient when bringing home a young African Grey; many do not begin speaking until age two, typically much later than other talking parrots.

African Grey (*P. e. erithacus*) and the Timneh (*P. e. Timneh*). Congos are larger birds, with bright red tails. Timnehs are smaller and a bit more delicate looking, with maroon tails. Some people have claimed that Congos make the better talkers, but since making such claims in print is guaranteed to generate lots of mail from indignant Timneh owners, I will not pick favorites here. Members of both subspecies possess the ability to become excellent talkers, given the proper training.

Like many intelligent beings, African Greys tend to be exquisitely sensitive creatures. Although I'm sure there are exceptions, most Greys like a calm household and a peaceful routine. My feeling is that they do best in one-bird and perhaps one-pet families, where they can be the secure center of love and attention. Unfortunately, because these birds can be such magnificent pets, owners often catch "parrot fever" and decide to add too many other birds to the home too fast. Many aviculturalists believe that Greys are particularly upset by noisy, rambunctious Amazons. Certainly, I have encountered a number of Greys who began to featherpluck upon being forced to share their home with another parrot. Once they begin plucking, it is very difficult to convince them to stop.

Amazons, which are known to be capable talkers, are more likely to thrive in a busy or rowdy household than some other birds.

Because African Greys tend to like a quiet environment where they can be the center of attention, they may do better in one-pet households.

You should also be aware that African Greys start to speak at a later age than any of the other talking parrots that we'll discuss. Many Greys don't say a word until age one and a half or even until age two. It makes sense that an intelligent animal would take a bit longer to develop than a less intelligent one, but it can be frustrating for the human who goes months without any feedback from the talking lessons. I can only advise you to be patient and to keep talking to your young Grey. You may not believe it, but your feathered friend is hanging on your every word.

AMAZONS—PARROTS THAT PARTY

If you worry that your household is too rowdy for the sensibilities of an African Grey, you may want to consider one of the Amazon species. These parrots tend to be adaptable to changes in routine, capable of entertaining themselves, and cheerfully self-confident about life with a flock of other birds or pets. They can also be loud, attention-demanding talkers and/or singers. Their voices are not always as clear or as human as an African Grey's, but there are exceptions. A few years back, a minor scandal erupted when a television commercial producer dubbed over the voice of a Blue-Front trained by Joanie Doss. The bird's real voice was said to sound too human to be believable.

Probably the most highly regarded talking Amazons belong to the Yellow-Crowned (*Amazona ochrocephala*) group, which contains several subspecies that make great pets for the active family, including such famed parrots as the Double Yellowhead (*A. o. oratrix*) and the Yellow-Naped (*A. o. auropalliata*). I've met many people who are absolutely convinced that the amount of yellow on the head of an Amazon tells you exactly how much talent the bird will have—the more yellow, the more talking ability. I won't try to analyze the logic behind this thinking, but I will point out that because these birds don't develop their full coloration until maturity, I think it's far better to begin training early rather than to wait and see how yellow a particular bird gets. Older Amazons who have never spoken are a lot tougher to train.

Double Yellowheads, as the name implies, gradually develop an entire golden head, which contrasts attractively with their green bodies. They seem to be the singers of the Amazon family, and whenever I'm told of a parrot that can sing entire human songs, it often turns out to be a Double Yellowhead. Yellow-Napes have a lovely yellow patch on the nape of their necks. Panama (*A. o. panamensis*) and Yellow-Fronted (*A. o. o.*) Amazons have a small patch or crown of gold on their foreheads. While Panamas and Yellow-Fronts are easily confused, the Panama is a smaller bird. Look for tiny white or clear "hairs" around the nostrils of a Panama, where a Yellow-Front will have dark "hairs." You should know what subspecies you have in case you ever decide to breed your bird, but I wouldn't be disappointed to learn that a bird purchased as a Panama was really a Yellow-Front or vice versa. Both can be sweet, assertive, and personable birds.

Of course, Amazons don't

Another member of the Yellow-Front group, the Yellow-Nape is a gifted talker and personable pet.

Double Yellowheads are skilled singers that have been known to sing entire human songs.

A domestic, handfed Amazon chick is the best option for a beginner who is looking for an Amazon to bond with, which is an important part of any training program.

have to be members of the Yellow-Front group to become talented talkers. Blue-Fronted Amazons (*A. aestiva*) are also very well regarded, and I can think of individuals of many other Amazon species that have proven to be very gifted. A beginner would be wise to select a domestic, handfed Amazon, preferably a chick that you can bond with. Because Amazons live a long time, there are still some older wild-caught birds around, and if for some reason you encounter one of these birds, you may find it difficult, if not impossible, to handle if it hasn't already been properly trained. An enraged Amazon, with beak ready to chomp, can be a formidable creature indeed.

Like all parrots, Amazons have their drawbacks. If you want a cuddle bird, you might not be happy with an Amazon, since they go through moods where they want their independence and prefer only to be scratched on the head instead of petted all over. Older Amazons can also experience hormonal surges that make them difficult to deal with during the breeding season, when they may bite their owners to "claim" them for their own. It's very important to establish from the beginning that you're the boss and that, although the Amazon is allowed to create a certain amount of noise and have his fun, there will be zero tolerance of biting and misbehavior. Ignoring bad behavior can be the worst punishment possible for an Amazon, a creature who thrives on attention.

It's also important to train these birds to ride on your arms, below the level of your face, instead of on your shoulder. (Yes, they're heavy. Just think of it as a weight-lifting exercise.) I find that if you can establish psychological dominance by keeping your head above the level of your Amazon's, you can remain in charge and keep the bird's personality sweet. Think of your Amazon's psychology as something like a small child's. The bird doesn't really want the responsibility for dominating

Like other Amazons, the Blue-Fronted thrives on attention and may test an owner's patience if not properly trained.

and directing the household. He just feels a playful need to see what he can get away with.

A SMALL SURPRISE—THE BUDGERIGAR

Here's a bird that makes it possible for just about anyone to own a talking pet. Budgerigars (*Melopsittacus undulatus*) are inexpensive, easy to care for, and come in a variety of delightful colors. Trained young, they can also display an astonishing ability to pick up human speech. According to *The Guinness Book of World Records 1998*, a Budgie named Puck had the largest vocabulary of any bird—1,728 words. I have heard unsubstantiated claims of Budgies whose vocabulary exceeded 2,000 words. If you have an exceptionally talented Budgie, it might be worthwhile investing in a tape recorder, so that you can document your pet's abilities for the record books.

Many people firmly believe that only a male Budgie will make a good talker. Others point to female Budgies that talk just as well. I would advise you to select a young, healthy Budgie that seems alert and interested in forming a bond with you. I cannot recommend that you wait until a Budgie begins to show evidence of its sex, because I firmly believe that a Budgie must be trained earlier if it is to become the best possible pet. You can identify young Budgies by the dark lines or bars on the crown of the head. As a bird matures, the bars vanish. In most color varieties, the cere will also change color, turn-

Budgies that are trained young make the best pets—and the best talkers.

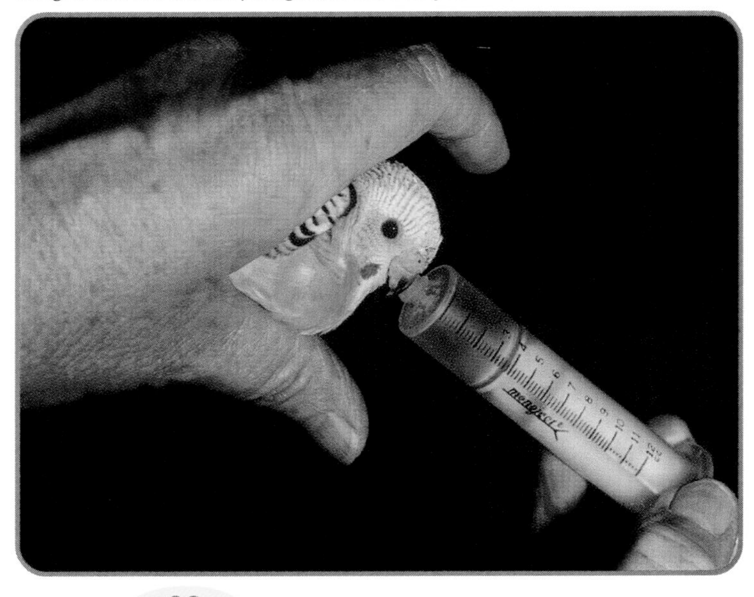

ing blue for a male bird and brown for a female.

You're unlikely to mistake a Budgie's voice for a human voice. Their powers of mimicry are somewhat limited. In addition to having what I can only describe as a chattery "parrot" voice, they tend to talk too fast. In order to encourage them to enunciate clearly, it is very important that you speak much more slowly and clearly than normal during training. That way, when the bird speeds up your voice, it will actually sound more natural.

Budgerigars, often commonly referred to as parakeets, possess a surprising ability to talk and are tolerant of learning from recordings.

ASIAN PARAKEETS—THE UNKNOWN TALKERS

If you want a sleek, handsome talker, you can't go wrong with the Asian parakeets that belong to the Psittacula genus. These elegant birds include the Indian Ring-Necked Parakeet (*Psittacula krameri manillensis*), which comes in a variety of attractive color mutations, including some gorgeous shades of blue. Others include the African Ring-Necked (*P. k. krameri*), the Moustached (*P. alexandri*), the Alexandrine (*P. eupatria*), the Derbyan (*P. derbiana*), the Plum-Headed (*P. cyanocephala*), and the Blossom-Headed (*P. roseata*). Psittacula species have been admired for their beauty and talent for thousands of years, and I'm not sure why

A bird's environment is extremely important to its well-being. A well-designed cage will be spacious, with properly placed perches and food and water containers. Photo courtesy of Animal Environments.

The Asian parakeets of the Psittacula genus possess many of the same speaking skills as the better-known Amazons and Greys.

they're not as well known to the public as the brash Amazons or the gifted Greys.

As with Budgies, don't wait until you can determine whether the bird is male or female. Although some people claim that you have a better chance of getting a great talker if you start with a male, your very best chance of getting a fantastic talker is to start training early. Psittacula are among the group of birds being reported to sometimes start speaking even before they're weaned, so it's obviously never too early to start greeting and speaking to these avian beauties.

Psittacula species can be a great choice for someone who doesn't feel up to the rambunctious personality of an Amazon, yet who is hesitant to cope with the delicate sensitivities of a Grey. The Psittacula species seem to be more tolerant of change than a Grey, with an Amazon's ability to amuse itself when you have to be away at work. And, while I never advise anyone to select a bird to match one's decor, there is no overlooking the fact that these birds are among the most eye-catching around. Some of the blue varieties of the Indian Ring-Necked Parakeet are truly among the most beautiful birds in the world.

A potential problem that you may encounter is that many people don't consider Psittacula species to be pet material. As a result, breeders often raise the birds only as aviary specimens, instead of handfeeding them for the pet market. This becomes a self-fulfilling prophecy, since the parent-reared birds are indeed more likely to be wild and disinterested in human companionship.

Although Scarlet Macaws have been known to speak a few words, they are best chosen for their other attributes.

The Indian Ring-Necked Parakeets are capable talkers, though handfed pets can be hard to find.

WHAT ABOUT MY BIRD?

Again, you shouldn't presume that your bird will never talk just because it isn't on this list. There are individual birds that can speak from virtually every species of parrot. In general, if no member of a parrot species has ever learned to talk, it's a pretty good assumption that it's a rare or perhaps endangered bird that has never been available for this sort of training. Like people, parrots are individuals, and an individual of talent or even genius can crop up where you least expect it.

Cockatoos, which sometimes annoy owners with loud squawking, can actually have pleasant and appealing speaking voices.

To avoid disappointment, however, let me dispel the misconception that macaws and cockatoos tend to make excellent talkers. These beautiful birds look good in advertisements and television programs, and it's only natural that an advertiser would use the striking image of a talking scarlet macaw to sell a product. In general, however, these parrots aren't as verbal as the Greys or the Amazons, and they tend to learn only a few words. Cockatoos often have a clear, sweet speaking voice, but they tend to use it rather sparingly—in contrast with their loud, raucous squawking voice, which they can sometimes overindulge in. I'm not saying that these birds lack intelligence, because anyone who has dealt with them knows that they are extremely intelligent. What I am saying is that they should not be purchased with the idea that they will become champion talkers, because it's unlikely to happen unless you stumble onto an exceptionally verbal individual.

The pet bird you choose should first and foremost be chosen as a companion, not as a performer.

GETTING STARTED RIGHT

Before you commit to bringing home a pet bird, you need to educate yourself about that species' particular needs, so that you will be able to provide the right food, housing, and general care for your pet. Dozens, if not hundreds, of books have been written on the different types of parrots, and it would be impossible for me to include all of the information you'll need to know in one volume. Read other books and magazines, discuss your plans with experienced bird owners and breeders, and take your time selecting the right pet for your family.

If you want a well-trained talker, please be patient and wait until things are relatively quiet at home and at work before purchasing a new parrot. Those precious first few weeks set the stage for everything that you will accomplish with your bird in the future. In fact, if you miss that window of opportunity, you may never be able to properly tame certain birds. Budgies, in particular, must be educated while still young or they become unbelievably difficult to work with. Greys can develop unnecessary fears and pluck off their feathers if not offered loving reassurance. Any parrot that is naturally vocal may develop a bad habit of screeching to get your attention if you haven't taken the time to channel his energy into talking or singing.

You will find it easier to teach a parrot to talk if the bird is already tame. Although it's true that there are many reports of untamed parrots learning to talk, your pet has a lot more motivation to want to impress you or please you with speech if he already feels safe and loved in your presence. Parrots live a long time, and though the overwhelming majority of parrots being offered for sale today are domestic-bred, handfed babies, it is possible that you may encounter an older wild-caught bird being offered for sale. My advice is to allow a breeder to purchase the older bird, especially if he's at all untame. The handfed baby will cost a bit more, because you are paying for the labor involved in feeding the youngster around the clock and

Have fun with your training. Time spent teaching your parrot to talk should be enjoyed by both of you.

A tame parrot is more likely to respond to your efforts to teach him to talk than a parrot that has not been tamed.

Handfed, domestic babies, such as these one-month-old Congo African Greys, make ideal candidates for speech training.

teaching him to enjoy being handled by humans, but it will be well worth it.

I must warn you that I have heard occasional complaints of "puppy mill" type operations, where a human handfeeder raises the bird but spends little time handling or talking to it. In my experience, most people who raise birds get into it because they love parrots, not because they're

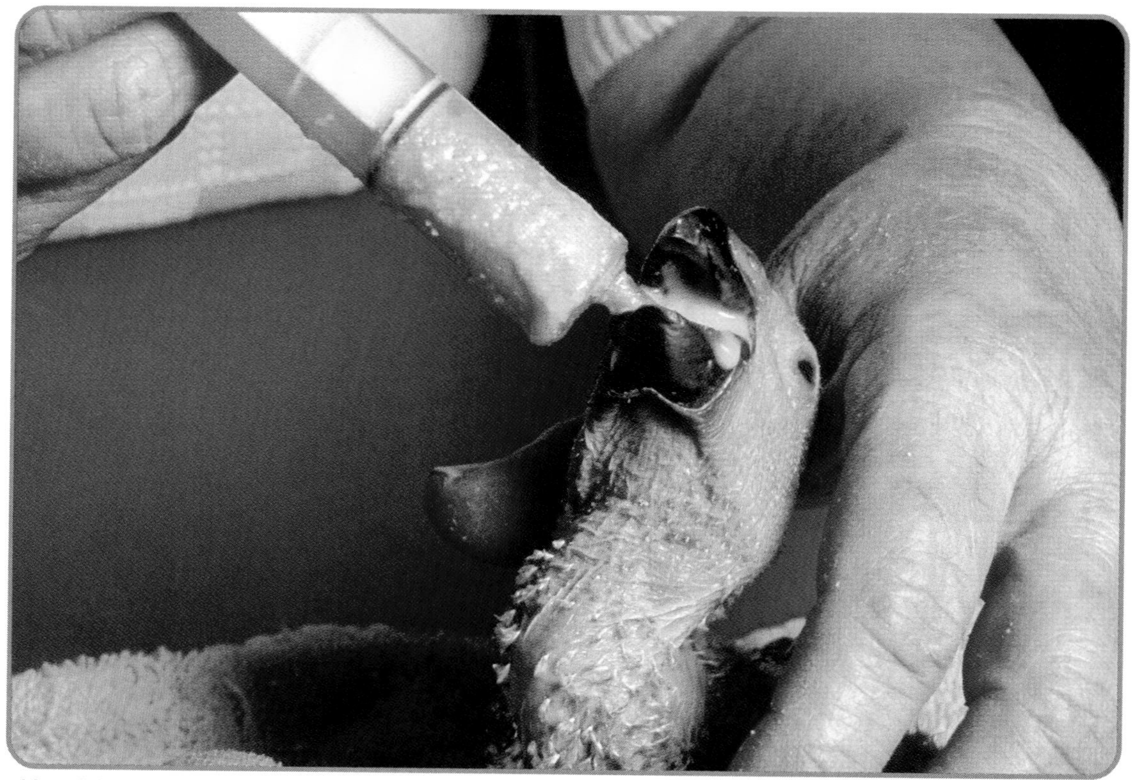

Although handfeeding can help with bonding, it does require a good deal of expertise and time. Consider a young, weaned bird as an alternative.

wild about climbing out of bed in the middle of the night for spoonfeeding. I believe that the majority of bird breeders are extremely conscientious people who know that you should demonstrate love and tenderness to a baby parrot, not just an ability to handle a feeding syringe. However, to dispel any doubts, get that vet check and also study how the bird reacts to human handling. You want a pet that is confident and alert, yet relaxed around people. The baby that catches your eye and tries to snuggle or even chatter to you is probably the right bird for you.

As your parrot matures, you should continue to develop a trusting relationship with him. One way is to include playtime with training.

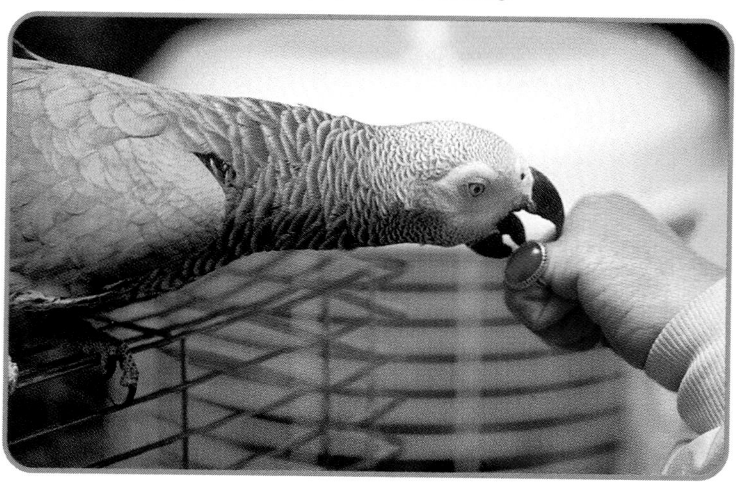

Some breeders will make unweaned baby parrots available for sale, explaining that they will teach you what you need to know to finish handfeeding your new pet. The advantage here is that you can bond with your parrot earlier, getting the ultimate early start on a good relationship. There may also be a reduction in the price, since you'll be doing some of the work yourself.

Five-week-old Senegal Parrots. Finding a young parrot will not guarantee you a chatterbox, but it's a step in the right direction.

However, at the risk of alienating some very sincere people, I can't honestly recommend such an approach to the average person. Handfeeding requires a certain touch, which I would hate for you to learn at your parrot's expense. Beginners sometimes starve a baby by unintentionally underfeeding it. They can also overheat the food, causing them to burn a fledgling's crop so badly that it requires surgery. Additionally, it can be difficult for the first-timer to properly wean a parrot, and some birds will take advantage of this situation, demanding to be handfed for months more than are really necessary. It's one thing if you're interested in eventually raising birds yourself, because everyone has to learn sometime, and there's probably no better place to do it than under the eye of a more experienced breeder. However, for most of us, the best choice will be a young bird that is just weaned, rather than a bird that still requires handfeeding.

It may take some patience for your parrot to speak its first word, but other words should soon follow.

THE FIRST WORD

According to surveys and my own experiences, the most common word spoken by a parrot is, "Hello," and the most popular sound effect is still the good old-fashioned wolf whistle. Why? Probably because this word and this sound are the two most common noises that humans make whenever they approach a parrot to make it speak! We will try to be a bit more imaginative.

I would advise you from the very beginning to banish the wolf whistle and the sound of any whistling at all from the home. There is an old saying that a bird that learns to whistle first will never get interested in learning to talk, and I think there's probably a lot of truth to that, at least for many parrots. Whistling is so easy and can claim so much attention that a skilled whistler might never develop any motivation to speak his very first word. In any case, it does no harm to put off the whistling lesson until the parrot can say at least a few phrases.

It is natural to start the lesson with a greeting, and "Hello" is probably as good as any. However, some people have theorized that Budgies and possibly some other parrots have trouble with the sounds "l," "m," and "n" when they're first learning to speak. "P" and "r" are supposed to be

Be cautious with any bird's tendency to whistle rather than speak. Whistling, which comes easily to many birds, can often get in the way of talking.

Good nutrition is essential for successful training. Gourmet treat diets may attract finicky hookbills with colorful fruits and vegetables and hearty nuts and seeds. Photo courtesy of Sunshine Bird Supplies.

Although some birds may train better when out of their cage, the presence of other birds may prove distracting.

easier to pronounce. Therefore, I always start by teaching "Pretty bird" when I am working with Budgies or other small hookbills. I've also noticed that, when a bird is learning "Hello," it often sounds a bit like a blurred mutter at first, which is not necessarily encouraging to beginners.

Of course, you don't have to start with "Pretty bird," but I like the idea of catching your novice talker's attention with a short, rhythmic phrase. When a new talker is in the mumbling stage, it is easier to pick out a three-syllable singsong from his usual chatter, which will let you know that you're actually getting somewhere, so that you don't give up just before you would have broken through and achieved success. I used to recommend that owners start with a one-syllable word such as "Hi," but I have changed my mind. The one syllable word may be easier to say in theory, but three syllable phrases don't seem to be any more difficult in practice. My Budgies certainly had no trouble learning "Pretty bird" first, and surveys suggest that just as many, if not more, birds say "Hello" and "Pretty bird" than the shorter "Hi." "Hi there" or "How ya doing?" might create more rhythm than a simple "Hi" and thus capture your pet's attention faster.

Have you decided who will be the parrot's primary teacher? There is usually one person in the family who is most interested in working with the bird and who will be in charge of the voice lessons. Many people believe that the majority of parrots will learn most easily from a person with a high-pitched voice—a woman or a child. Be aware that if the child is very young, a good mimic will slur his words just like the child's. Cookie sometimes drops his voice very low to speak just like his former owner's grandchild, announcing that, "I'm gonna cry." On those occasions, his voice is soft, childlike, and truly indistinguishable from a three year old's. He speaks in his former owner's clear, crisp voice when using that individual's favorite catch phrases, "That'll work" and "Nothing wrong with that."

There is no real scientific proof, but I tend to agree that most parrots, especially Budgies and Amazons, can be fascinated by high-pitched or even falsetto voices. I have heard numerous stories about Amazons that are fascinated by opera sopranos. However, some people believe that African Greys are more attracted to deeper male voices. In practice, of course, you'll end up working with whatever voice you happen to possess,

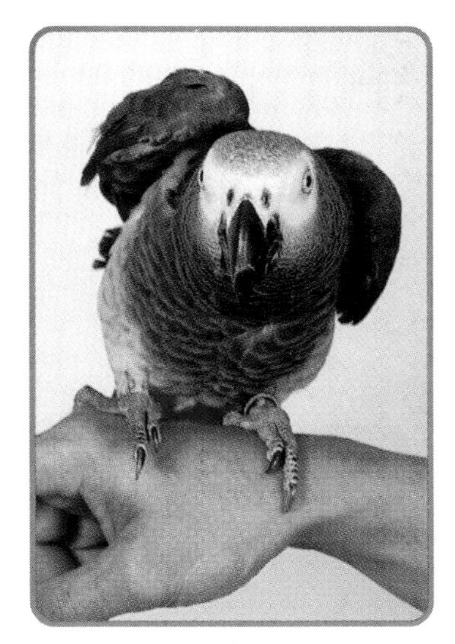

Consider which member of your family will be the primary trainer. Many believe that Amazons and Budgies learn best from high-pitched voices, while African Greys do better with deeper voices.

Many birds are quite capable mimics and can duplicate the exact pitch and style of different voices and even of doorbells and barking dogs.

but it's good to get others in the household interested. Keep everyone up-to-date on what the "phrase of the week" is, and get family members in the habit of using the phrase appropriately around the bird. After all, until you try, you'll never know whose voice will best capture your pet's attention.

THE FIRST LESSONS

Repetition is the key to success in teaching a parrot to speak. You can give your hookbill a wonderful home and a loving environment, but the bird won't necessarily be inspired to talk about it unless you make it very clear what you're after. Yet you have to work within your pet's attention span, which is as limited as that of a small child. I will confess that my personal attention span is also pretty limited when it comes to perching a bird on my arm and repeating "Pretty bird" for a half an hour at a time. I feel that several short five-minute sessions scattered throughout the day are a lot more effective than one marathon hour-long session once a day. I'm less likely to get bored and to communicate that boredom to the bird, and the parrot seems more alert and interested too.

Should your pet be caged during the training session? I think that you should use whatever method allows you to provide the greatest focus on the business at hand. When training hand-tamed Budgies, I like to lift them on my finger and bring them right up to my face, where they can watch my lips forming the words. Even though Budgies don't have lips and can't imitate my motions in order to imitate my words, I feel that I can capture their attention a little better this way. It is rather disconcerting to be repeating a silly phrase such as "Pretty bird" or "It isn't easy being green," only to watch your pupil very seriously pick up his latest toy and bash it about.

With larger birds, it can be easier to leave the parrot in the cage during the lesson. I like to partially, but not completely, cover the cage during the lesson, making a sort of tent out of the covering so that the hookbill is drawn to the open side of the cage, where I am speaking. Some people believe that you should completely cover the cage or even place it in total darkness during the voice lesson. In this way, the bird will have nothing to concentrate on except the sound of your voice. Please don't try it! You will be forever sorry if you teach your parrot to associate talking with darkness. After all, you will want to sleep sometime, and the sound of a demanding bird calling, "Hello, hello, HELLO!" is far from a peaceful lullaby.

Some owners find that training works best when their parrot is left in his cage, away from household noises and distractions.

African Greys, thought by many to be the most intelligent of parrots, must be given creative outlets for their talents. Take advantage of your Grey's skills and communicate with him as often as possible.

Be aware of other noises that are going on in the area during the lessons. Is there something you've tuned out that the parrot will pick up on? I lived to regret playing a parrot teaching tape only during my morning shower. I didn't realize until it was too late that the Peach-Fronted Conure taking the lesson only attempted to speak when the water was running. And "Hello" is not a particularly appropriate response to a rainstorm or a shower.

Of course, you should speak clearly and not mumble when training a parrot to talk.

Contrary to popular belief, cockatoos—like macaws—are generally not champion talkers.

Tune into your bird's attitude during training and watch for signs that he's had enough for the day.

Unless you speak loudly and clearly and with some degree of enthusiasm, the bird is unlikely to pick up the phrase. As I mentioned in the previous chapter, a larger hookbill will learn to mimic you exactly, but it can be very important to exaggerate the pronunciation and to *slow* your speaking voice when training a Budgie. For some reason, these birds will naturally speed up whatever they're taught, and if you yourself talk too fast, what you'll hear will be a blur.

If you work during the day, you're probably wondering when you'll be able to provide those several five-minute lessons during the work week. Actually, you can fit the lessons into your schedule quite easily. When you get up in the morning and feed the bird, it's natural to greet your pet and spend a few moments talking to him. When you come home in the evening you will find that your bird again expects to be greeted, presenting another occasion for a quick but meaningful lesson. Later in the evening, work in a few more lessons. Don't get stressed about it. Make it a normal part of your interaction with your pet. Give yourself permission to relax and enjoy this marvelous creature you've brought into your life.

Mynahs, though not part of the parrot family, are considered to be among the best avian talkers.

Before beginning training, think carefully about the words and phrases you'll use in your lessons. You're likely to hear them many, many times.

You may experience the most exciting results if you place the current lesson in context. Say that you're starting off with the phrase "Pretty bird." This phrase can be a very valuable and thrilling one for a parrot, because it can be used to draw attention to the bird, thus securing it praise and admiration. When you get up in the morning, say very enthusiastically something like, "Well, hello there, pretty bird!" before segueing into the lesson. Again, when you come home, greet the bird, tell him how pretty he is, and then sort of slide into the repetition. Make the lesson all part of a friendly game between the two of you.

If you mindlessly and mechanically repeat a phrase out of context, the parrot may very well learn to say that phrase, but he doesn't get the opportunity to associate any meaning to the words and the whole experience won't be quite as special. I've made my share of mistakes in the past, when I labored under the assumption that birds couldn't really understand. Teaching the Conure that "Hello" was a way to announce that I was in the shower was admittedly pretty silly. And I've certainly been guilty of teaching a Budgie to prattle "Pretty bird" without the slightest notion of what he was saying or that it could be considered praise from a human being. I happen to find the mindless chatter of a Budgie quite soothing, but it's still a bit more interesting when a bird is obviously speaking in order to spark a human reaction.

It may take a while for your parrot to speak words clearly. Be patient and be certain to enunciate and repeat words often.

We'll talk more later about how to help your parrot understand what he's saying. For now, keep in mind that it's a good idea to use language, even repetitive language, in an appropriate setting.

ELECTRONIC HELP

If you persist in giving about 30 minutes worth of lessons a day, in sessions of about 5 or 10 minutes each time, you may be pleasantly surprised at how fast your bird begins to respond. Or you may not. A naturally talented bird might begin to speak right away, especially an Amazon, a Budgie, or one of the Psittacula species. However, what if you have an African Grey, that may not utter a word for a year or more? Or what if you have an individual, of whatever species, that might need a bit more training before it catches on? Or what if you're worried that your voice isn't high enough or enthusiastic enough or attention-getting enough? What if you start telling yourself that, just possibly, you're wasting your time?

It can be hard for the trainer to stay motivated week after week and month after month. Personally, I find it difficult to keep repeating the same phrase over and over. After a time, the words seem to tangle up in my mouth, until I can barely say them myself, much less teach them to a parrot.

That's where the miracle of electronics comes in. We're fortunate to have a wide selection of tools and resources to help us train our parrots. In the past, I used to record a phrase on a short tape, such as those sold for older answering machines. Then I would turn on the tape recorder when I was out of the house (or, alas, in the shower) and let the bird continue with his studies without driving me crazy. More recently, I discovered a compact disc that allows me to select whatever track I want, out of a selection of dozens of phrases, to reinforce my pets' lessons.

You may use a combination of tape recordings and CDs if you like. With the tape, you can record your own voice and your own choice of phrases. However, the CD has a decided advantage in that it has superior sound quality and doesn't seem to wear. I once made the mistake of using an older tape of a canary's song to train my English Starling. Alas, the human ear is too good at tuning out what it doesn't want to hear, and I didn't realize what was happening until the Starling began to sing to me in perfect canary—warbles, trills, tape recorder static, and all!

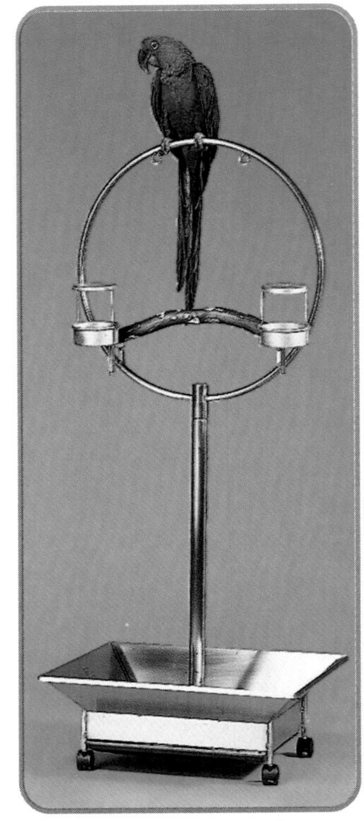

Ringstands provide birds with a place for perching and feeding outside of their cage; many owners find them an invaluable tool for training exercises. Photo courtesy of Animal Environments.

Although treats are an important part of training lessons, don't be too quick to reward your bird for every word spoken, every time.

Since I prefer to give speech lessons on a one-on-one basis, I haven't used the help of another bird to train my parrots. Many other people have, however, especially busy breeders with a number of parrots. Again, I wouldn't attempt to work with more than one bird if you're a beginner, but I'll concede that certain hookbills apparently do learn better if they see other birds talking first. Some resourceful trainers have even realized that a one-parrot family might benefit from a videotape that showed another bird talking. Although I haven't tried the videotape approach myself, I can confirm that my pets do react to television programs and that there's good reason to believe that such an approach can capture a bird's imagination. If your bird seems to enjoy visual stimulation and attempts to speak to pictures of other parrots in books or on television, why not give it a try?

The main problem with electronic devices is that they lend themselves to being abused. I believe that a lesson is most effective if it lasts about 20 minutes at a time. However, since even 20 minutes of "Polly wants a cracker!" is enough to test the patience of the average human, some owners have a tendency to leave the tape

Many owners tire of repeating the same words and phrases over and over. Tapes and recordings can be effective with some birds.

Certain birds, such as Budgies, do better with recorded lessons than others. However, recordings should not replace the interaction between you and your bird.

recording on while they are out. That works fine if they're running around the block to the store. But it isn't fine if they're going to be gone for an hour commute, an eight-hour workday, and an hour drive back. By then, even a so-called birdbrain has either learned to completely block out the sound or he has plotted his revenge. Amazons, in particular, aren't always shy about expressing their displeasure with a pinned eye and a dangerous beak.

Ironically, the one exception is the Budgie. I've had fairly good results with these birds by just leaving the tape recorder on and forgetting it. I think they incorporate it into their usual chatter and don't get so upset about the relentless nattering. After all, in the wild, they would be in huge flocks where they would be exposed to continuous Budgie chitchat. However, Amazons and other parrots seem to appreciate a certain amount of downtime during the day. The seemingly endless repetition can grate their nerves just as it grates ours.

Of course, you shouldn't use electronic devices as a substitute for personal training. You still need to work with the parrot yourself, so that the bird will learn to use speech to communicate with his human. Otherwise, you run the risk of creating a secret talker, who may very well chatter away for his own entertainment when no one is home but who won't utter a word when people are present.

KEEP UP THE GOOD WORK

One day, it happens. It may come out of the blue, when you're watching television or discussing the day's events with your family. All of a sudden, a demanding little voice will cry out, "Pretty bird!" Conversation will stop and everyone will look around to see if anyone else heard it too. For a moment of stunned silence, nobody speaks. But then everybody starts talking at once, in tones of amazed excitement, and the voice comes again, louder this time, "Pretty bird!"

Or it may come slowly, with a teasing buildup. For several days, you've noticed that the bird has been muttering to himself, perhaps stopping self-consciously when he notices you're listening. Once, when you're in another room, you're almost sure that you heard something. You don't want to say anything to anyone else, just in case you're wrong. Then it happens again, and the voice seems a bit more distinct. Could you be imagining things? Finally, when you least expect it, the parrot shouts out, "I love you!"

Training should become part of your daily routine with your pet; many find that feeding time is ideal for practicing words or phrases.

Those first few words are the sweetest—so sweet that some of us tend to lose our motivation to continue with the lessons. We have what we wanted. We now officially own a Talking Parrot. After all, if someone asks if our bird speaks, we can honestly say, "yes," without bothering to add that all he says is his own name. Yet, now that you've had the breakthrough, you might well have the ability to teach your pet dozens if not hundreds of phrases. You'll never know just how talented your bird truly is unless you give him a fair chance to keep learning.

However, don't rush ahead with the lessons too soon. When a bird is first learning a word or a phrase, it's appropriate to praise him with attention and even a food treat, even if the phrase isn't all that distinct. After all, we as proud owners can understand what the bird is saying, and we're just so thrilled. That's fine, at first. The bird needs and deserves the praise to keep him motivated and to let him know that he's moving in the right direction. After a time, though, you should no longer reward the bird or give him any special attention unless the phrase is said properly and clearly. You would be amazed at the sweet, clear speaking voices that many parrots are capable of if they are only given the right guidance.

Finish the first lesson before hurrying on to the second. Don't shortchange your parrot by assuming that a mumble is all that he's capable of. Many if not most parrots will mumble when they're first learning a phrase. It's a great sign that you're about to achieve success, not that you've got a talent-free bird. Do pronounce the phrase as clearly as you can, perhaps exaggerating just a little to give your pet the idea. Within a very short time, as long as you don't give up, you'll have a parrot with a speaking voice that can be understood by even the most skeptical listener.

Then, once your bird has learned his first word or phrase, start working on the next. I'm convinced that many parrots speak only a few words because their owners were satisfied with teaching it just a few. Give your bird continual opportunities to learn and you may be amazed at the size of the vocabulary that your pet eventually develops.

Rewards come in many forms besides food treats—extra scratches, attention, toys, sprays, and your time.

A PARROT THAT KNOWS WHAT HE'S TALKING ABOUT

I've tried to encourage you to train your bird to actually communicate with you, as well as to just repeat certain sounds for the sheer fun of it. When you wish to teach a new word or phrase, make a concerted effort to teach the phrase in a meaningful context. We've already discussed "Pretty bird," and how to teach your bird that this phrase is a charming way to ask for attention and admiration. It's also fairly easy to teach the basic greetings, such as "Hello" and "Good-bye." Most parrots seem to understand that "Hello" means something like, "I'm back, I'm glad to see you, and I'll be around for awhile." Being generally gregarious animals, they seem to greet each other with their own social noises in the wild, and some variant of "Hello," "Hi," or "How ya doing?" comes naturally to them. Indeed, you can expect to trade "Hello's" back and forth several times when you first get home. Enjoy the pleasant ruckus, because it's your pet's way of letting you know that it's great to be with you.

If you've ever doubted a bird's ability to understand, teach your hookbill about the word, "Good-bye" or "Bye-bye." Use the same phrase consistently whenever you leave the house, rather than, "See ya later" on some occasions and "Good-bye, honey," on others. After a time, the parrot will figure out that the phrase means that you're going out for awhile. How the bird uses this information depends on his individual personality. Some pets will cheerfully bid you, "Bye-bye," and get back to the serious business of destroying all the wooden toys in their cage. I have heard several reports of parrots who always use "Good-bye" in its proper context and who do not resort to emotional blackmail by saying, "Hello?" in a hopeful tone to convince you to change your mind. However, my birds are not among them.

Many owners find that training results are best when birds can concentrate on the movement of their owner's mouth as words are spoken.

Your parrot needs not only a well-balanced diet but healthy treats as well. Treats should be loaded with your pet's favorite fruits and nuts that offer nature's goodness in every bite. Photo courtesy of Sun Seed Company, Inc.

I suppose that a hard-headed scientist would point out that I can't really know what's going on in a parrot's brain and that it might just for some mysterious reason be incapable of processing the meaning of the word, "Good-bye." Maybe so, but I doubt it. In my experience, when a talking parrot is tired or grouchy or just not interested in human attention, he doesn't seem to have much trouble suddenly recalling the word. Cookie is happy to tell certain visitors, "Bye-bye," a not-too-subtle way of suggesting that he'd like to be alone with me. Very occasionally, when he's overtired or vexed with me, he'll tell me, "Bye-bye." Most of the time, however, he would prefer that I stay home—and, as a result, I've probably heard him say "Hello" thousands of times for each time he's said "Bye-bye." A parrot may not always succeed in manipulating his owner with language, but you can't blame a bird for trying!

As you go about your speech lessons, you may feel tempted to reward your bird with certain treats whenever he learns a new phrase. If you want your parrot to have some understanding of the meaning of what he's saying, you should only provide food treats when he talks about food. Dr. Pepperberg explains that, as part of Alex the African Grey's training, he's given whatever he asks for—grapes if he says "grapes," something to chew on if he says "cork," a caress if he says "tickle." As a result, he can develop clear and consistent associations between saying certain words and receiving certain forms of attention.

Although I don't know who originally trained Cookie, I can tell that he received a loose form of such training. When he wants something to eat, he says, "Polly wants a cracker, cracker, cracker!" When he's thirsty, he asks for a Coca-Cola, his word for water and all other liquids. Of course, calling all food "cracker" and all liquid "Coca-Cola" is not an especially correct use of the language, but it does get the point across. I suppose if you wanted to safeguard your reputation as a scrupulously responsible parrot keeper, you could teach your bird to say, "Polly wants a broccoli!" and "Gimme a bottled mineral water!"

In any case, if your parrot starts talking about food, by all means, feel free to reward him with some healthy food. If, however, he's talking about the weather, don't form a false association by popping a peanut in his beak. Try to develop consistent habits to go along with the consistent phrases that you're trying to teach. Although I'm not saying that the whole house should be at the beck and call of a pet parrot, do give the bird the admiration he's seeking when he is first learning to say an attention-getting phrase such as, "Kiss me, I love you," or "Watch the birdie, the pretty birdie." A bird that's ignored will, too often, either fall silent or learn to demand attention through the unattractive method of shrieking.

Give careful thought to the words that you use when you have to correct your parrot. When you say, "No," or "Bad bird," in a serious tone designed to get your pet's attention, your hookbill could be learning the words at the same time that he learns about improving his behavior. The one phrase that I object to hearing addressed to a talking parrot (or even to a human) is, "Shut up." Therefore, I'm always careful to use the words, "Hush" or "Shhhh" when my birds are too loud. These words, with their soft hissing sounds, can capture my pets' attention and cause them to lower their voices so they can hear exactly what I'm saying. Cookie does know how to say "Shut up," as I learned one day when he

Healthy food treats can be used in training lessons to associate specific words and phrases with the actual objects.

became upset that I was spending too much time on the telephone, but he has used the phrase only once in several years. I would hope that he's now forgotten it after all this time without hearing it.

"No" and "Bad bird" are, by contrast, useful phrases that give your bird a chance to vent. Cookie can always be relied upon to call out, "Bad bird" if one of my other birds somehow gets loose from its cage. Many people report that one pet bird will tattle on another bird, using the phrase "Bad bird" if they see their companion getting into mischief. Sometimes, if you do something to displease the parrot, such as trimming those long toenails, you may well find yourself addressed as the "Bad bird."

Don't pressure your bird to perform at all times. Learning to talk should be fun, not work.

THE MODEL/RIVAL METHOD

Consistent repetition is the heart of any speech-training program. However, there's a more advanced way to train your parrot to associate the proper words to the proper meanings—the model/rival (M/R) method used by Dr. Pepperberg and her associates to teach Alex and their other research parrots. It's a very effective but very time- and labor-intensive technique for training a bird to understand what he's saying. You should not feel bad about yourself or your bird if you decide the M/R technique is too much work for you. As I said before, your parrot doesn't have to learn to give interviews to television reporters to make a loving, responsive pet. It is better to enjoy your bird as he is than create a stressful situation for you or your family. Remember that Alex is a research bird and not a pet, and there are several trainers available to work with him at any given time.

As the name suggests, the model/rival method requires the use of a second person to play the role of the bird's model and rival. As a model, the person appears to be another student who is learning the lessons that you would like the parrot to learn. As a rival, the person represents a competitor for your attention. Inevitably, the bird will attempt to get your attention away from that person and back to himself. You will grant that attention and praise when your pet uses words appropriately, answering questions or making comments about the situation at hand. The technique can be used both to

In the event that your bird won't speak or you don't have time for him, consider finding him a mate or another bird to keep him company.

The model/rival approach used by Dr. Irene Pepperberg with her famous African Grey "Alex" may be a method to try with your own Grey.

teach new concepts and to improve pronunciation.

Let's say that you wish your bird would pronounce a certain phrase more clearly. At a time when the parrot is alert and interested, your partner will come into the room, and you will start to rehearse that phrase with the partner. If the partner slurs the word, you may say, "No!" or ignore the person for a few moments. When the partner pronounces the word correctly, you may praise the person or "reward" them with an appropriate prize, such as giving him a bit of peanut after they correctly say, "Give me a peanut."

In Alex's case, his trainers have modeled some fairly sophisticated concepts. He has been taught to count a few numbers, to recognize colors, and to answer questions about such concepts as size or shape. You'll probably want to model some less ambitious behaviors, at least at first. Suppose you would like to teach your bird to tell you when he wants to chew paper, rather than just going after the nearest library book. Therefore, you should set up some sessions with your partner that involve paper. Get some colorful pieces of paper and show them to your partner. When your partner says, "Give me paper," you could do so, and the partner could pretend to thoroughly relish the act of shredding it up. If your partner says, "Polly wanna cracker," you could say, "No!" and put the paper out of sight.

Be sure to switch the roles around, so that the same person doesn't always play the part of the student. You want the parrot to get the idea that different individuals can ask for paper or crackers or whatever—leading to the idea that the parrot himself can make specific requests. Say your bird has now tentatively asked, "Give me paper?" Even if the words are not perfect, if it is the first time, do reward the bird with the paper! As he chews to his heart's content, say something like, "That's good paper" or the like, to reinforce the association of the word "paper" with that delightful shredding.

One of Alex's rewards is quite imaginative and may actually seem a bit abstract to appeal to a bird's mentality, but apparently it works out quite well. Dr. Pepperberg explains that, as a research animal, Alex is often requested to answer questions about objects that don't really interest him all that much. Therefore, as a reward, he's allowed to ask for another object if he responds to the questions correctly. For

Instead of using the same kind of food treat over and over, consider tailoring the treat to the specific phrase or word spoken by your bird.

instance, if he says, "I want grape," he gets the grape only after he's answered his question correctly and properly requested the grape. He doesn't get a grape at random as a reward for answering a question that has nothing to do with grapes at all. And he doesn't get a grape simply by ignoring the task at hand to shout, "Grapes, please!"

Bird owners make a mistake when they assume that a parrot should receive an edible treat as a reward for learning every new trick or phrase. There are a lot of possible rewards—our attention, a toy to chew or destroy, a spray shower (particularly beloved by Amazons), even an enjoyable piece of music. When I think of how frequently some of us reward our parrots with the same food, no matter what they say, it's a wonder that our birds don't think that almost any word in the English language is slang for "pizza!" Try to fit the reward to the situation and you have a better chance of encouraging your parrot to associate the correct words with their actual meaning.

A parrot's diet, as well as that of other birds, should consist of a wide variety of seeds, fruits, and vegetables. For added nutrition, many seed diets are fortified with vitamins, minerals, and amino acids. Supplemental products are also available to keep your bird healthy. Photo courtesy of Sun Seed Company, Inc.

Like any other training technique, the M/R method will have to be applied consistently if you wish to see results. The two trainers involved don't always have to be the same two trainers, but someone should be working with the parrot every day. Unfortunately, if one person is "assigning" the tasks of play-acting with the parrot, while others think the concept is silly or just feel foolish acting out the role of student in front of a pet bird, I don't think you can expect the excellent results that Dr. Pepperberg has demonstrated. You need at least two highly motivated humans in the household to use this method of training, and you need the patience to act out roles that may seem rather ridiculous at first. Laugh, enjoy yourself, and make the ongoing sessions fun both for family members and for parrot. If the training sessions become a miserable duty, neither bird nor partner is going to be motivated.

SINGING AND WHISTLING

Once your pet is chattering away, you may decide that it's time to take the next step. You may teach your bird to sing, to whistle, or to do both. I generally make a distinction between the parrots I would select for song training and the ones I select for whistling. When working with an exceptionally talented talker with a clear voice, I might try to prevent my student from hearing anyone whistle, even on recordings. In that way, I can channel the bird's energy toward learning to sing in human language. With less talented talkers, I might encourage whistling because it's an area where the pet can shine, even if he never becomes any great conversationalist.

The Cockatiel is one good example of a sweet, popular parrot that rarely learns to speak well. One in a hundred or even less might be a spectacular talker. Yet many of these charmers can learn to whistle quite well, even without formal training. If you own one of these birds and you're becoming discouraged

Allow your pet's true talents to shine through. If your Cockatiel is a great whistler, but can't speak a single word, let him whistle.

by a lack of progress with speech training, I see no harm in switching to whistling lessons. The bird might not ever learn to talk, but you'll both enjoy hearing him whistle a happy tune.

Other parrots, such as the Double Yellowheaded Amazon, demonstrate such talent that it would be a shame to divert their gifts to mere whistling. Many Amazons thoroughly enjoy the process of learning to sing. You train such birds much as you would train them to talk, with the added attraction that the natural rhythm of the song will help capture your pets' attention. Teach one line of a song at a time, gradually adding on as the parrot learns. Amazons, Greys, and even Budgies have learned entire songs, a truly impressive accomplishment.

There are many people that can neither sing nor whistle. Here is where electronic devices are worth their weight in gold. Just don't make the mistake that I did, of using an old, staticky tape, because birds do repeat *everything* they hear. There's little thrill in training your parrot to mimic the skips in a defective CD!

Once your bird has mastered talking, consider teaching him to sing songs. Amazons, in particular, love learning to sing.

SOLVING PARROT PROBLEMS

I will be the first to admit it. There are going to be times when you wonder why you went to so much trouble to teach your parrot to speak up. Talking parrots don't tend to be shy, retiring creatures. As a general rule of thumb, you can assume that a bird is interested in learning to talk, sing, or whistle because it's a fairly vocal specimen of the species. In other words, talking parrots can be astoundingly loud.

When people complain about screaming pets, I first check to see if they have realistic expectations. One man came to me in distress because he said that he couldn't sleep due to his "noisy, shrieking" Fischer's Lovebirds. I later acquired the birds and satisfied myself that they were actually very quiet animals. This man made two mistakes. The first was that he placed the cage between his bed and his south-facing window, which caught the rays from the early morning sun. When the sun came up, the Lovebirds greeted it with their usual chatter. Their "noise" was

Parrots that are good talkers can also be good squawkers. Yelling back may only encourage more noise.

Parrots will generate a certain amount of chatter as well as occasional calls to greet one another.

actually nothing out of the ordinary, but he had a resentful attitude toward it because it awoke him at dawn. The second mistake is that he simply had an unfair concept of how little noise a parrot can be expected to create. Secure birds do chatter amongst themselves. Only a very fearful, insecure bird would never dare to utter a sound.

In general, parrots will vocalize in the morning, as a way to greet the sun and salute the new day. They'll usually call to you regularly when you're in the house but out of sight. They'll also tend to get a little loud and enthusiastic about greeting you whenever you return from work or other absences. In the wild, parrots would constantly be greeting each other in the morning and as they rejoin the flock. Certainly, when a mate or flock member is out of sight, they would call back and forth to make sure everybody's safe. You aren't going to be able to maintain a hushed, library-like silence in the home and also be the proud possessor of an excellent talking parrot. However, you can learn to recognize these normal interactions and how they differ from obnoxious screaming.

Like it or not, many parrots will scream, at least a little bit, when you first leave the house. They simply don't want you to go. I wouldn't be offended by such a display of affection. If you're concerned that your parrot is shrieking the whole time that you're gone, you can experiment by parking your car down the street and sneaking back to the house. You will probably be amazed to discover that your parrot is perfectly quiet and content, having the time of his life playing peacefully with his toys—until he realizes that you're back within guilt-tripping range. If a parrot is in fact screaming by the hour, this behavior is definitely abnormal and needs to be dealt with immediately.

Some parrots are such social animals that it's truly a hardship for them to be left for hours without any companionship. Many Cockatoos fall into this category, which is why I tend to recommend them only to families where someone is at home most of

Some parrots, despite your best efforts, will not talk—at least in your presence. Consider using a tape recorder to see if your bird is a "secret talker."

the day. All parrots require some companionship and attention from their owners, however, and I would ask you to look at your schedule very carefully to make sure that you aren't neglecting your pet. A parrot isn't a mechanical device that runs on a daily change of paper, food, and water. It needs love and attention, too. Fortunately, when you commit to daily speech training lessons, you are developing the habit of incorporating your pet into your everyday life.

Other parrots scream because they're spoiled. Some people even unintentionally train their pets to scream. It's only natural to come running when you hear a bloodcurdling shriek from your feathered friend. Often, these shrieks are a signal that you're needed and that something is seriously wrong—a mouse in the room, a toenail caught in a trap, or a broken blood feather. However, a good amount of shrieking is performed for the express purpose of making a human run and for providing the bird with a good laugh. This is the sort of shrieking that you want to discourage, and the best way to discourage it is to give no reaction at all.

Remember when we discussed the fact that a human's attention can be the best reward of all for a parrot? Well, when you scream, "Shut up!" or dash panic-stricken into the bird's room, you're providing a form of attention just as surely as when you lavish praise on your pet for saying "Pretty bird." It's negative attention, but it's dramatic and apparently highly amusing to the devious psittacine mentality. Every time you overreact to your pet's shrieking, you reinforce the idea that he can create drama simply by raising his voice.

Cockatoos require a good deal of human companionship and will be quite clear about letting you know when they feel neglected.

I would never tell you to ignore your pet if you have the slightest doubt about his safety. If that screech sounds sincere, check it out. However, I'd like to assure you that, over time, you'll learn to distinguish between a genuine distress call and an attempt to play with your emotions. I've been complimented on my (reasonably) quiet birds, but for some reason they do enjoy seeing me chase cats out of the yard. For a time, the Conures had me convinced that they were genuinely terrified if they could see a cat anywhere in the neighborhood, even though there was no way that the felines could reach their aviaries. As a result, I found myself being called out to chase cats at least once or twice a day.

Parrots enjoy combinations of seeds, nuts, and fruits; fortunately, they're available in a range of treats and regular diet combinations. Photo courtesy of Vitakraft Pet Products Co., Inc.

A parrot that has health problems or plucks his feathers will generally be less inclined to learn to talk. Consult your vet with any concerns.

As time passed, however, I noticed that there was a definite difference in their calls on those occasions when they really needed my help and the times when they'd just like to see some cat chasing. The "cat here" call was a bit less strident, with an air of saving their voices so that they could keep on calling until I'd broken down and responded. The fear just sounded a bit more genuine when they had an actual problem to contend with. I then discovered that if I simply ignored the "cat here" call, the Conures would give up and stop calling me. At first, the birds fussed even louder, con-

Toys and other distractions can prevent your bird from reaching his true talking potential. Take a look at your bird's surroundings to see that he has a good learning environment.

vinced that I would respond if they just insisted. Over time, however, I basically broke them of the habit of announcing every cat that passed by. The house and yard are a lot quieter, and I've only found myself chasing cats once in awhile.

Finally, be aware that parrots tend to vocalize more in a noisy environment. If your house is filled with screaming children, a blaring television, heavy metal music, and a ringing telephone, it's unrealistic not to expect the bird to chime in. Also, be aware of any ambient noise that you may have learned to filter out. Is there construction work going on in the neighborhood? I always know about it first, because Cookie is eager to help out, not only by flirting and attempting to get the attention of the crew, but also by vocalizing with various sawing and hammering sounds. If you're aware of what's encouraging the bird to shout, you might be amused, rather than upset—although I admit to being a bit embarrassed when a roofer told me that he hadn't realized for a couple of hours that it was a parrot heckling and whistling at him!

THE SILENT BIRD

Not all parrots are overly vocal. In fact, many people complain that their pets are too quiet. I always recommend a vet checkup for a new pet parrot so you can be sure he isn't suffering from any health problems that may affect his desire to talk. Also, be aware that some birds will stay quiet for a few days while they're adjusting to their new home. If a bird that previously spoke well suddenly falls silent, another health check is in order. Your vet is the best judge of whether your parrot has acquired a problem that's draining his energy.

Of course, many birds are healthy but simply choose not to talk. Perhaps the most frustrating problem is the

Some parrots may be more likely to talk when there is some background noise or activity, rather than when they feel pressured to perform.

bird that knows perfectly well how to speak but won't utter a word in front of friends and family. If you hear your pet muttering to himself from another room, only to have him clamp his beak firmly shut whenever humans are present, you may well possess a secret talker. Why not leave a voice-activated tape recorder in the parrot's room to verify your suspicions?

Some birds seem to feel it's rude to mimic you to your face. I've been told that Cookie can do a perfect imitation of my voice, but I'm not allowed to hear it. I do know that he does a great imitation of his previous owner—who in turn has not been allowed to hear that. Perhaps such parrots feel that mimicking "the mommy" would be a challenge to the owner's loving authority. In that case, you would do well to provide other voices for the bird to mimic, including other family members or voices on various recordings. Whenever the bird does speak, make a special effort to reward him with praise and attention. You may wish to start with a food-oriented phrase, such as "Polly wants a cracker," so that an appropriate reward for speaking would be a favorite treat.

Be careful, a talking bird may repeat anything. Your sweet parrot may surprise you with occasional bouts of foul language if exposed to it.

If a lack of confidence is what's stopping the bird from speaking in your presence, you may want to consider the location of the parrot's cage or playpen. As a general rule, the "top dog" in any avian society is the bird that perches the highest. I mentioned earlier that you should work to keep Amazons or other potentially aggressive hookbills off your shoulder and on your arm so that they are below the level of your face. In this manner, you establish who is in charge in the household. However, if your pet seems unusually timid or insecure, you may want to make some adjustments. Raise the cage or playpen and see if the bird gains confidence. It seems like a small thing, but it can make all the difference in the world. Of course, if a hookbill decides that he's now the dominant member of the family, you'll need to lower his perches again. It's amazing what a little fine-tuning in its altitude can do for a bird's attitude.

The best defense to your bird's inappropriate language is to ignore it. Any other attention may only encourage him.

Some parrots seem to use speech only as a way to keep in touch when you're out of sight. You may be able to encourage these birds to talk back and forth with you by responding with conversation from the next room. You may feel a bit silly, shouting "I love you" back and forth to a pet in the next room while vacuuming the carpet, but rest assured that your hookbill is enjoying the game—and getting more confidence in his use of the language. Sometimes you can encourage these birds to speak while you're in the room by partially covering the cage. Don't be afraid to experiment a little.

Other parrots chatter away in front of family members but quickly quiet down when you're trying to show off their talents to outsiders. Remember, a bird wants your love and attention, not that of a stranger. The best way to encourage these pets to talk is to go on socializing with your friend, without paying much if any attention to the bird. Let your parrot take his time about observing the situation without being stared at. Personally, I've discovered that a heated political discussion can usually excite the bird enough to get him to weigh in. Just as you're completely caught up in some all-important debating point, your pet is likely to sing out a loud, commanding, "Hello, pretty bird!"

Most parrots like to have a little noise in the background to encourage them to speak. In the wild, the jungle or forest tends to fall completely silent only when somebody has spotted a predator. If everyone else is keeping quiet, instinct shouts that the parrot should stay silent also. A good way to encourage your bird to talk more is to have some sort of white noise going, such as running water or even the vacuum cleaner. You'd be amazed at the number of hookbills that talk up a storm while people are cleaning the house.

If your home is extremely quiet, you can't expect your parrot to talk as much as he would in a noisier environment. There's a fine line we have to walk between encouraging our birds to shriek and encouraging them to fall completely silent. I wouldn't leave the television on all day, but there's nothing wrong with playing some dramatic music like opera once in awhile to stimulate your feathered talker. I also like to play a recording of "rain forest" sounds because I think it inspires my birds to vocalize a bit more.

"BAD" WORDS AND SOUNDS

After going over how you'll need to train your parrot to speak, I have to reveal that it's possible for a bird to learn to repeat a phrase after hearing it just one time—especially if it's the phrase

To visibly improve color and vitality, trust your bird's diet to thoroughly researched and quality-tested foods. Ask your veterinarian about specialty care diets that are also available. Photo courtesy of Roudybush, Inc.

Training is not a short-lived activity. As he matures, your bird will continue to appreciate any time spent with him learning new things, including new words and phrases.

that you shouted when you hit your thumb with the hammer. Unfortunately, just as other dramatic, rhythmic words capture your pet's attention, obscenities and profanities tend to register immediately in the avian mind, probably because these words are said with such force. Once your bird has the gift of gab, you have to assume that he can pick up anything he hears. To avoid teaching him the wrong thing, you may have to make a concerted effort to watch your language.

A few people may say that they refuse to be shocked by "mere words." I've even met the occasional owner who has deliberately taught the bird to repeat certain taboo phrases. I'd like to remind these owners that many parrots, particularly Amazons, can be expected to live for decades. By teaching the bird naughty language, you may have inadvertently closed some doors in the bird's future. What if you decide to have children and realize that you don't want to expose them to a foul-mouthed bird? What if you become ill or even die and someone else has to find another home for your pet? Can you honestly state that you believe a cursing parrot has the same chance of finding a good, caring home as a non-cursing one?

Since we're humans and not angels, it's normal to vent once in awhile. If at all possible, you should probably try to replace certain forbidden words with more acceptable language. Admittedly, this can lead to hilarious results. Cookie, whose previous owner also had a small grandchild in the home, picked up the word "poo-poo" as the ultimate insult. When he's vexed, he may call you a "big poo" in the child's voice. And when he really wants to load it on, it's, "I'm gonna cry, big poo. Big poo-poo!" Silly as it sounds, it's a lot better than the alternative. In fact, we generally all laugh—the bird included.

Given that we sometimes slip up, the parrot may eventually hear and even repeat a taboo word. The best way to deal with the situation is to ignore it. Don't give your pet any attention, either negative or positive, for using the objectionable word. So-called punishment, such as spraying the bird with water or covering his cage, may just teach him that saying the word is a good way to get a shower or some fuss and attention. Although you'll be tempted to react, your best choice is truly to pretend not to have heard a thing. If the parrot can't associate a response to a particular word, he will have less incentive to keep using that word. Unfortunately, it may take a long time for the steel-trap avian brain to completely forget the word, but you just have to have faith that he will eventually turn his attention to other things. You'll have more success with this as long as you practice selective hearing and only reward your pet for saying other more desirable phrases.

Proper training requires that you assert authority over your pet. Birds that are allowed to perch on shoulders may feel more in control and less likely to behave.

MY BIRD QUIT TALKING!

Sometimes a good talker will suddenly start to mumble or even fall silent. In such cases you may need to perform a little detective work to get your bird back on track. As mentioned earlier, a parrot may not feel up to talking if he's undergoing a heavy molt or recovering from an injury or sickness. You don't necessarily know right away if your pet is feeling under the weather, because animals possess a natural instinct to conceal their illnesses. In the wild, a bird that looks sick draws the attention of predators such as hawks, which naturally wish to conserve their own energies by chasing easy prey. Therefore, I'd like to repeat my previous advice that you consult an avian vet

Learn to appreciate your bird's many assets. Even without stellar speaking skills, their antics can provide many hours of enjoyment.

if you can't see any obvious reason why your feathered friend is suddenly disinclined to talk.

Assuming your parrot has received a clean bill of health, let's look at some other reasons why your bird might have stopped talking. I've noticed that many Amazons, for instance, may go through cycles where they alternate speaking clearly and imaginatively for several weeks with periods where they prefer to mumble when not focusing on their favorite words. It isn't always easy to pinpoint exactly why a good talker that knows perfect pronunciation will go through weeks of muttering under his breath.

I believe that many of these cycles are related to changes in the home and family. Some parrots will become very quiet while they are sizing up a new cage, house, or family, and it isn't unusual for a new pet to be rather quiet when you first bring it home. Other hookbills, however, will react to their new people by trying on a variety of words and phrases, perhaps to impress their new owner and to ensure that they will be admired and well treated in the new environment. These birds are more likely to mumble when they're relaxed and settled in, because they're confident that they've already won your heart. Being kind and patient, and continuing to lavish praise where it's appropriate, is the best way to break through with both kinds of parrots.

Be aware that some changes that capture a bird's attention will seem rather minor to a human. It's easy to notice such major changes in the household as a child going away to college for the first time, an older family member moving in, or an unfortunate divorce. However, bringing home a new pet, whether another bird, a dog, a cat, or even an iguana, can upset a parrot's world. Hookbills tend to be very possessive of their owners, and while some birds will undoubtedly call and talk to you more in order to steal your attention from that new puppy, others are not above sulking for awhile. All you can do is continue to provide consistent love and attention, along with enjoyable speech training lessons.

Small changes in a favorite person's appearance can also have bizarre effects on a parrot. Hookbills often take particular notice when their human starts wearing glasses or changes a hairstyle. Although I've heard wild tales of birds angrily removing the offending glasses or curlers, I feel that you can prevent most of this behavior by proper training. Have you fallen into the bad habit of carrying the parrot around on your shoulder instead of on your arm? It seems so convenient, but if you keep your pet on an equal level with your face, you'll have a lot more trouble maintaining the proper authority. No wonder the bird feels free to reach over and restyle your hair.

Not all parrots react negatively to change, so maintain a positive attitude about the various happenings in your household. As intelligent, social creatures, birds tend to pick up on our emotions and perhaps magnify them a little. If we're upbeat yet relaxed, our pets will tend to react the same way. And don't take a parrot's opinion about the changes in your appearance too seriously. To date, Cookie has been most impressed by the time that I dyed my hair green for Halloween, reacting with an almost embarrassing storm of wolf whistles to the news that I suddenly matched the Amazon in the household!

A LIFELONG PROCESS

Of course, it's always possible that your bird is mumbling because you haven't been reinforcing his clear, correct speech. If you're a naturally quiet person, you may need to make an effort to remind yourself to speak to your parrot and to keep him included in the family conversation. Just as you did in the beginning, greet the bird in the morning and in the evening, and make a point of spending quality time with your pet as often as you can. Continue to play recordings of favorite phrases, as well as phrases that you might not hear as often. You never know what's going to spark the psittacine imagination.

There's also the possibility that you're exhausting your parrot by providing too much attention. In a loud, noisy household, it's easy to forget that the hookbill will do best with 12 hours of sleep a night. Have at least one quiet retreat in the home where the bird can sleep when the day is done. Try to sensitize yourself to the little signs that your pet is becoming cranky and in more of a mood to nip than to chat. Make talking a form of attention the bird enjoys, not an exhausting routine that involves showing off for the neighbors at all hours of the night.

As you make the fine adjustments to the household that will encourage your parrot to show off his talking skills, you may wonder when it's time to give up trying to teach your bird new things. Actually, you never have to give up as long as the two of you are both enjoying the process. Parrots can keep learning for their entire lives, so there's no reason for you to stop training your bird to pick up fascinating new phrases. According to reports, a Yellow-Naped Amazon said to be more than 100 years old and requiring about 20 hours of sleep a day still used his large and rather colorful vocabulary.

When you start to teach your parrot to speak, you've embarked on an enjoyable journey that will bond you more closely to your bird and teach you a little bit about how another creature thinks. Whether your bird is a gifted chatterbox or just likes to repeat the same few phrases, you can feel proud that you've had a part in educating such a delightful charmer. There's no reason to cut the process short just because the bird has reached a certain age. You and your talented talker should continue to appreciate each other for the next several decades!